peace breathing

peace breathing
lessons on achieving peace in everyday life

Dear Tim Suh,
with infinite peace and love.

Master Kim

Charles H.C. Kim

the peace ◉ school

Peace Breathing © Copyright 2012, Charles H.C. Kim
All rights reserved. No part of this book may be used or reproduced in any manner whatsoever without written permission from the publisher, except in the case of brief quotations in critical articles and reviews.
First Edition   ISBN 13: 978-1-937484-03-3
AMIKA PRESS   466 Central Ave #23 Northfield IL 60093   847 920 8084
info@amikapress.com   Available for purchase on amikapress.com
Edited by Jennifer Kim, Jenn Morea and Carol Stoker. Author photograph by Ron Wu Photo. Designed and typeset by Sarah Koz. Body in Oranda BT, designed by Gerard Unger in 1986. Titles in Stymie, designed by Morris Fuller Benton in 1931. Thanks to Nathan Matteson.

*In memory of my father, MyungSu YuSung Kim,
who tirelessly devoted his life to peace for humanity
and brought the gift of Peace Breathing to the world.*

contents

foreword by Li-Young Lee   **ix**
introduction   **1**

31 talks
  1   lessons of the ocean   **5**
  2   good or bad   **7**
  3   sharpening your focus   **11**
  4   let the sun shine   **14**
  5   new math for healthy relationships   **18**
  6   do me a favor   **21**
  7   the mountain and the tree   **23**
  8   closer each time   **26**
  9   the foundation comes first   **28**
10   reflections on water   **31**
11   the best recipe   **34**
12   accepting the unexpected   **38**
13   the island   **41**
14   you're the driver   **43**
15   practice, practice, practice   **46**

16	a balanced life	49
17	making a genuine connection	53
18	doing the dishes	56
19	healing our planet	58
20	finding your way	61
21	above and below	63
22	the bridge to your future	65
23	the clean-up	68
24	oranges and apples	71
25	individuals impact the world	73
26	washing your clothes	75
27	in harmony with the universe	77
28	a breakthrough	79
29	painting a clear self-portrait	82
30	embrace the energy of today	84
31	playing in harmony	88

peace breathing meditation   91
about the peace school   97

foreword

This is not primarily a book of ideas, thank goodness. Ideas, however profound and useful as some of them might some of the time be, have the unfortunate tendency to lag behind immediate experience, which occurs always in the present moment and in the consciousness of that moment, borne not, as some would believe, horizontally upon the wave of the expired past to rush headlong into a pre-determined future, but continually welling up, fountaining vertically from the obscure sources of life and breath itself. This book exhorts us to inhabit, fully awake, that crest of the fountain, the very lip of the breath-filled present, however beset by confusion, anxiety, doubt, and fear that moment may sometimes seem to be. For it is in the present that we breathe; it is in the present that presence is possible, that mindfulness is possible, and making enlightened choices of words and actions possible. This book proposes a reliable technique in order to remain present: Peace Breathing.

Resting the mind on the breath while repeating a mantra is an ancient method of calling the mind back to presence, written about in many Hindu, Daoist, and Buddhist texts dating back several thousands of years. And nowadays, there are plenty of books explaining in detail the health benefits of deep breathing, as well as the psychological rewards of meditation. But this book places that method in the context of everyday life, reminding us to practice and enact meditative presence, meditative awareness, in the real and ongoing world. But what is meditative presence? What is meditative awareness? At the risk of over-simplification, it is being present to our interconnectedness to all things. It is being aware of our intimate participation in a greater order of Being. Only by the deepest realization of these truths in our lives will any single one of us be capable of love and all of its forms: charity, sympathy, empathy, compassion, etc. No world, however small or large, is safe in the keeping of anyone who is incapable of love. By heeding the words in this book, may every one of us become a more loving individual, and may all worlds find safe-keeping with each of us.

—*Li-Young Lee*

introduction

This book is a collection of 31 talks that will open your heart to new possibilities for peace. Each chapter contains an important lesson which can be incorporated into your daily life. While it is possible to read the whole book in one sitting, the book lends itself to reading one chapter each day of the month. You can then spend the day contemplating and practicing its message. Carry the book with you to lift your spirits by reading a favorite talk when time allows. Be sure to refer to the Peace Breathing guide found on page 91. If you practice Peace Breathing as you read this book, you will surely grasp the deeper meaning behind the simplicity of each story.

31 talks

1 ● lessons of the ocean

Some people think of peace as being weak or passive. But that's not correct. Peace is strong. It is like the ocean which is able to remain calm at its depths even when there are storms on the surface. When a storm occurs, the ocean may be rough on the surface with waves that are 30-feet high, but if you go much farther below, it's calm and consistent and not impacted at all by what is happening above.

No matter what happens on the surface of your life, maintaining that deep calm is so important. If you have a shallow perspective when stressful situations occur, you will feel as if you're being tossed by the ocean's waves as your emotions go up and down. How many times do you try not to get upset? You think, "Don't do it, don't do it," but you still do. Or you might not even think about it and just automatically have a negative response. When you're stressed, you feel tense and tight and your breathing becomes faster. Stress blocks the flow of energy and can make you feel overwhelmed. If your mind is like the ocean's surface with 30-foot waves going all the time, you can't see clearly. To avoid that, slow down your breathing and think of the calmness of the ocean's depths. This will help open your mind to new possibilities and ways of approaching your situation, when only a few minutes ago you felt out of control.

Peace is not only strong, it is big and expansive enough to accommodate all. That's the power it has. It's like the ocean. When we look at the ocean, it's so big that we can't even see how far it goes. It's vast and therefore able to provide a home for diverse sea life and is a destination for the many rivers that flow into it. Expansion of energy in our daily lives makes it easier to work with any type of person or situation. We are no longer disturbed by others even if their energy is rough. In time, we willingly accommodate others, creating a more peaceful environment for them and ourselves.

In order to bring about peace, you don't have to do anything extraordinary. You are a true peacemaker when you use your daily life to express harmony and love. Expanding your energy to make the best of each moment helps you to become more peaceful day by day. Other people start to naturally fit into your world. You have the capacity to create a smooth energy exchange, touching the hearts of others, and providing hope and encouragement. Without even realizing it, you have an influence on your family and friends, your workplace and your community, and ultimately the world. Like the ocean, your vast energy is strong, helping you create a calm and peaceful life that is truly enjoyable, and each new experience only adds to your fulfillment and growth.

2 ● good or bad

As a child growing up in Korea, I remember hearing a story that has always stuck with me. It was about a certain gentleman who lived in a village bordering two rival areas within old China. This particular man owned a horse, which was a valuable commodity in those days. One day his horse disappeared across the border. Neighbors came to him, saying how sorry they were about his loss, expecting to hear more about his troubles. But all the man had to say was, "We'll see." The neighbors thought this was odd. He didn't seem to be at all upset about losing his prized possession.

In time, the man's horse returned and brought with it a female companion. Neighbors came by to heartily congratulate the gentleman on his good fortune. Not only did he get his horse back, but he now had a female horse as well, so that he could breed the horses in the future. What great luck! They were completely surprised when the man, showing no excitement, calmly responded the same way, saying again, "We'll see."

Later, the man's only child was riding the new horse and fell, suffering a severe leg injury which caused him to be crippled for the rest of his life. When this happened, many people gathered at the father's home to express their great sorrow and anguish over his only son's misfortune. *How could such a terrible thing happen? If only that female horse had never come.* But with no sadness or worry on his face, his only response was still, "We'll see." The people of the village shook their heads, completely baffled by his calm reaction to this devastating accident.

Then war broke out across the border. All the young men of the village were called to war, and nearly every single one was killed in battle. The man's son, however, was not required to join the fighting because of his crippled leg. Thus, his life was spared. At that point the villagers began to understand the wisdom of the man's perspective. Instead of judging each circumstance as good or bad, he accepted each situation as it was. He maintained a calm and even temperament, trusting that there was a reason behind every event. The villagers gained new respect for his peacefulness, vision, openness and trust.

In our own day-to-day lives, we are often quick to make judgments: *That's great! Oh no, too bad! I love it! I hate it! What a good experience! What a terrible experience!* If we take some time to think about it more deeply, we can see that each and every experience has its own value. It all depends on how we utilize the many things that occur to us in a day, in a year, in a lifetime.

When a so-called bad experience happens, it often leads us to a new life direction. It can open our eyes to something we had not considered. It can take us out of our daily routine and make us look at the bigger picture. It can help us to see someone in a different light. It can direct us to search for the meaning of our lives. So, in the end then, is it really a bad experience?

When a so-called good experience happens, we can re-create it in our minds over and over again, eventually living in the past instead of the present. We might continuously compare our daily life with the memory of the good experience. Our family and friends tire of hearing about it. We feel disappointed when other experiences are not as good as that particular one. Then, is this good experience really good for us?

From a lifetime perspective, there is no such thing as a good experience or a bad experience. It is only our small viewpoint at a given moment that makes the judgment of good or bad. If we open our minds and consider a wider perspective, we can see each one as it is, just like the others. Instead of reacting to each experience, we can see every occurrence as part of our learning process and personal evolution. If we can be grateful for any experience and try to learn from it, no matter how it may seem in the moment, we will move through life smoothly, with more consistent energy, and find the place of real happiness within ourselves.

From this perspective, all experiences can be thought of as stepping stones which lead us toward a brighter future. This is because the universe is moving toward harmony and expansion. As our minds become steadier and more open, we naturally tap into the beautiful energy that is always flowing around us and within us. We feel our connection with each other, with nature and with all of life. Most of all, it helps us to see ourselves more clearly, to realize that the bright, expansive harmony exists within our own hearts. By staying in tune with this harmony, we are not swayed by events or circumstances. Instead, we are able to get the most out of each moment of our lives.

3 ◉ sharpening your focus

A magnifying glass is great fun, especially when you're a child. You become a detective, examining tiny objects and fine print. It makes you laugh when you magnify your own finger or a friend's nose. But the greatest surprise comes when you take it outside in the sun and carefully hold it over a small piece of paper or dry leaf. Incredibly, it becomes hotter and hotter until the paper or leaf starts to burn. This works especially well when the magnifying glass has been cleaned beforehand.

As the sun's rays pass through the magnifying glass, they join together and become focused on a single point. It is this concentration of the sun's energy that makes the difference. More than just creating the visual effect of enlargement, an actual increase in power has taken place. This same principle can be helpful as we engage in our daily activities, conversations, tasks and studies.

When our lives are busy and our minds over-loaded, it's easy to give only fleeting attention to various things throughout the day. Add to it the tendency to get pulled into things that don't necessarily have anything to do with our own lives, and we can see how easy it is to lose focus.

For example, we may spend a lot of time thinking about the details of an experience from our past, or having long discussions about other people's business, or making critical judgments about things we may know little about, or worrying about an illness that we don't even have. This scatters our energy, giving us less time and energy to focus on what is really important. Even the most basic things we need to accomplish might be overlooked. Our bigger goals and dreams could then drift into the background until they have been forgotten.

So, how can we bring our life back into focus? Instead of scattering our attention in many different directions, we need to learn how to pinpoint our focus, like the magnifying glass, toward today's activities, conversations or thoughts. Furthermore, we need to find a way to keep our larger dreams and goals in the picture, ideally incorporating them into our daily living. Of course, this takes practice. It helps if we have an easy method to keep us from being distracted by unnecessary thoughts and activities. We also must get used to keeping the mind steadily focused on what we are doing at the moment and seeing how our daily thoughts and activities contribute to our bigger goals.

Peace Breathing is a way to keep our lives in focus and eliminate the non-positive things that scatter our energy. This is like cleaning the magnifying glass, making it easier to keep the mind focused and in the moment. Peace

Breathing also keeps us in touch with the larger goal of working toward peace for ourselves and for others.

By putting this or other similar methods into practice on a consistent basis, our power increases like that of the light passing through the magnifying glass. We find that we have much greater energy and power than before. This translates into heightened creativity, more compassionate listening, quicker and more thorough work results and greater focus. This gives us the satisfaction of knowing that we have done our absolute best.

4 ◉ let the sun shine

What a welcome sight it is to see the sun! Particularly after a day or two of cloudy weather, we all seem to perk up when the sun comes out. The enormous energy, warmth and brightness of the sun seem to naturally lift our spirits.

The light of the sun is a constant in our world. Although sometimes obscured by clouds and sometimes hidden from us on the other side of our planet, the sun never ceases to shine brightly, expansively, equally. In the world of the sun there is only bright light and powerful energy in every direction. At any given moment there is a dark side of the Earth, a dark side of the moon, but who ever heard of a dark side of the sun? There is no such thing.

What does human existence have in common with the sun? If we think about this, we can find an important connection. Let's first think of an object that does not shine by itself, like a planet. No matter how close it may be to a light-generating object such as the sun nor how bright the sun may be, the planet will always have a bright side and a dark side. Likewise, when we rely on an outside source for our own happiness or improvement, we will have a bright side and a dark side to ourselves. The person or source we rely on may be beautiful, bright and pure, and we may thoroughly enjoy basking in the glow of the light-filled energy they create. Yet, something is missing. For all the bright energy we may experience through an outside source, a part of us will still be in the shadows. And, when we are away from that bright person or outside source of light, we are left in the dark again. We must strive to create the bright energy by ourselves, to become a light-generating entity just like the sun. If we ourselves become bright, we will no longer have a dark side or even the hint of a shadow.

We can learn from what we see and admire in others, but instead of relying on other people for our own development, we must reach deep inside ourselves to find the beauty and brightness we so admire. Instead of depending upon a teaching or philosophy for our betterment, we must find a way to make those ideas our own by actively expressing them in our daily lives. Then, that bright and powerful energy will start to grow inside of us. Even though our efforts may seem small at first, it will only be a matter of time before we reach our goal, as long as we continue to work toward it.

Peace Breathing is a tool that we can use to brighten ourselves. Peace Breathing harmonizes our breath with our thoughts and actions, ultimately creating the bright energy of peace as a foundation for our daily lives. With each breath, the thought of "World Peace" generates the energy of peace and harmony. This bright energy impacts us first and then expands widely to others. With continued practice, every breath becomes light itself.

Without energy, nothing forms—not the physical body, nor thoughts, nor any material objects. Our lives are the result of the energy that we ourselves have built up over time. In order to become bright within, in order for us to shine like the sun, we need to concentrate as much as we can on expressing only bright energy through our daily lives. Rather than practicing hard one day and skipping the next, consistent daily practice is the quickest way to move forward. The more consistent our practice, the more we can avoid frequent ups and downs, and the smoother and more stable our transition will be as we change and improve ourselves. Through regular, steady practice we can eventually keep, and ultimately expand, that bright energy within us at all times.

Some people we meet make us feel off-balance, uneasy, sometimes even fearful. Other people naturally cheer us up, emitting a bright feeling of warmth and genuine kindness. These same people are often able to maintain their positive nature even when confronted with heavy negativity. These are the people who have found a way to brighten themselves like the sun. We should reflect on what it is that people feel from us. Is it positive? We must realize that the type of energy we generate is purely our own decision. Whether positive or not, the energy we create will have a direct impact on our own future, on others and ultimately on the future of humanity.

With bright energy we can reach out beyond the limitations or boundaries that have held us back in the past.

With bright energy we touch the hearts of everyone with whom we come in contact and live in harmony with all of nature. We may think that it's not possible to live this way with so much conflict and stress in today's world, yet at this very moment there are people among us who are truly shining like the sun itself, ever bright and expansive.

We have much to learn from the sun. For all its energy, for all its warmth and brightness, for all our dependence upon it for sustaining life on our planet, the sun never asks for our respect or longs for recognition. The sun never shines on those it likes and denies its light to those it doesn't. Moment by moment, the sun pours out its vast energy and far-reaching light without hesitation, pride, judgment or expectations. The people who are most like the sun are those who live brightly yet quietly, living for the benefit of others. Unwavering and consistent, they are full of life and energy, never ceasing to shine, yet modest by nature. This could be you—this could be any one of us. Those who make this their goal and put it into practice on a daily basis will surely succeed. Each one of us has the ability to express the same bright, expansive qualities of the beautiful sun.

5 ◉ new math for healthy relationships

One plus one equals… Even small children know the obvious answer: two. But could it ever be possible for one plus one to equal less than two? More than two? When we think in terms of the energy exchange between people, our take on this firm mathematical rule begins to shift.

When two people work together, live together or have lives otherwise intertwined, an exchange of energy between the two is always taking place. Each person brings to the relationship their own unique characteristics based on their past experiences, likes and dislikes, talents and shortcomings, and the extent to which they are open to the viewpoints of others.

When two people have sincere respect for each other and wish for the other person's happiness, they tend to feel great whenever they are together. When unrealistic expectations, resentment, jealousy, or annoyance start creeping in, both people come away feeling dissatisfied. Put another way, being with someone with whom we share respect and support gives us an energy boost, while being with someone with whom we don't get along is a drain on our energy. The energy of two people can be greatly enhanced and expanded through their relationship, so that each person becomes more than what they were individually. On the other hand, when there is conflict in a relationship, it causes a depletion of energy in both people.

It takes effort for two people to develop a positive relationship, and a good relationship cannot be forced. After all, everyone has good points and not so good points, and we have a choice as to what we focus on within ourselves and what we see in the other person. We can make the choice to focus on everything that is wrong with the other person, and it can be easy to justify this type of thinking. But we tend to forget that by focusing on the negative, we're taking away rather than adding to the energy exchange. If we prefer to have positive, energy-building interactions with others, we can start by keeping our own thoughts bright and open to possibilities. If we make the effort to look at the big picture, to understand the other person's perspective, and to respect a different point of view, we are on the path to deeper communication, and we experience an increase of energy.

Most of us live hectic lives, but it is still important for each of us to set aside time for ourselves to look inward. Methods such as meditation, prayer, affirmations, or Peace Breathing help us stay on the right track not only within ourselves but in our relationships with others. These types of methods help us to create energy which is bright and uplifting—energy that expands—making it natural for us to be open to others. Rather than working against each other, working together becomes the norm. Thus, the equation of one (you) plus one (me) can equal more than two or less than two, depending on the positive or non-positive energy we exchange.

6 ◉ do me a favor

A friend has been getting his home ready for a big event and is putting the finishing touches on the yard. He is pressed for time and asks if you can help by planting a new bush out front. Proud of your gardening skills, you look at the spot where he wants the bush planted and answer, "Sure, I'll do it first thing tomorrow morning." You notice a small rock in the soil but think nothing of it.

You arrive the next morning as promised feeling eager to accomplish your task. You start to dig, but your shovel hits something solid. You try another spot but your shovel stops again. You get down on the ground and start poking around to see what the problem is. Then you realize that the small rock you noticed yesterday is actually the tip of a bigger rock under the soil. You dig and dig until you find that the rock is huge and too heavy for you to deal with by yourself. You're frustrated because you thought this was going to be a quick and easy job. You look at the time, realizing that you have to get to work. You're upset when you leave, not sure when and how you can finish. Your friend is unhappy, too. You seemed so sure you'd have the bush planted today, but instead you left his front yard a mess. Your attitude is, "Hey, I was trying to do you a favor." His attitude is, "I thought you knew what you are doing."

People casually ask for favors, and people casually agree. These conversations are usually based on what can be seen on the surface. Your friend knows you're a gardener so he assumes you can plant the bush in no time. You take a quick look at the area and assume the rock you spotted is insignificant. If either one of you had given yourselves time to think, you might have considered the consequences if anything went wrong. You might have paused to assess the situation before saying you could do the job. If you had literally dug deeper and found the huge rock hidden below the surface, both you and your friend could have avoided the difficult situation and hurt feelings.

When a friend asks for a favor, it is hard not to readily agree. In fact, we sometimes agree to do a favor, rather than say no, just to avoid feeling uncomfortable. Yet it would be better to go through this momentary discomfort before agreeing to something we might not be able to accomplish. In the end, your friend will be truly grateful that you took the time to dig deeper and that you both were able to avoid a worse situation. Deeper energy will help you look into a situation more thoroughly and help prevent the kind of issues that drag you both down.

7 ◉ the mountain and the tree

Mountains give us a wonderful chance to experience the magnificence of nature. It is a rare person who is not touched by the beauty and power of a mountain. Mountains can inspire us, refresh us, challenge us and fill us with awe. After centuries have passed, a mountain may eventually deteriorate, but when it is fertile it is full of life. The tiniest seed, dropped by a passing bird or carried by the wind, can grow into a beautiful flower or a strong tree on a mountain. Such a mountain provides a nurturing environment, giving plants the energy they need to flourish. The plants, in turn, add to the beauty of the mountain. More than this, the mountain receives an enormous benefit from the plant life it sustains.

But what if a mountain somehow decided that it wanted to keep all of its energy to itself? What if it grew resentful of the plants covering its surface and withheld its energy from them? From the smallest weed to the tallest tree, one by one the plants would wither and die. Even the strongest tree would be unable to grow without support from the mountain. The mountain would then be free from having to support the plants. Does this mean that the mountain would end up with more energy for itself than before? Would the mountain really be better off?

As the hot sun beat down or heavy rains fell or high winds blew, the mountain would find itself in a much more vulnerable position than before. A lush, green mountain has the capacity to withstand extreme conditions due to the benefit it receives from plant life. The intricate root systems of small plants hold the topsoil in place, while larger plants and trees are deeply rooted in the ground. A barren mountain is likely to experience destructive flooding and mud slides or be worn away by wind and sun. Rather than gaining energy each day, this mountain would become weaker and would soon meet its own destruction because of its refusal to share its energy.

Of course, a mountain would never deny its energy to plant life. But when we think deeply about the relationship between the mountain and the plants, we can see how the sharing of energy causes the total energy to increase, not decrease. As the mountain "gives up" some of its energy to support the plants, it gains much more in return. The life of the mountain is enriched and ultimately sustained because of the energy it provides to the plants. This is one example of the great harmony of nature. If we think about the relationships we have with others, we can see how the same rule of harmony in nature can be applied to human existence.

Do we often reflect on our own wants and needs, yet give only passing attention to the needs of someone else? Have we grown accustomed to protecting our own interests, dismissing or justifying the effects on others? Do we focus on our immediate benefit without considering the long-term consequences of our actions? Do we insist on getting our own way? If such habits have become common, we may be moving in the direction of the mountain that refuses to share any of its energy. We may think that we are better off if we concentrate on "taking care of number one." After all, this seems to make perfect sense in today's world. We can find all kinds of reasons to believe in such a way of living. But in the long run it isolates us and drains our energy. It is unlikely that we will be able to achieve real happiness or fulfillment with such an outlook. We can see the result of self-centered thinking in personal relationships as well as in global situations.

On the other hand, if we are open to others and willing to share what we have, we give others a comfortable feeling. People go out of their way to help us whenever the need arises. By sharing our energy with others we gain deeper satisfaction and genuine happiness. Our lives move in positive directions because of the bright energy we created, and our days are further enriched by the bright energy reflected back to us from others.

We can't expect to achieve harmony in one day, but rather through a consistent daily practice such as Peace Breathing. In time we will create sustaining, life-enhancing energy for ourselves and for others, just like the mountain and the tree.

8 ◉ closer each time

Thomas Edison failed hundreds or perhaps thousands of times before inventing the light bulb. Time after time his light bulb prototypes didn't work, until finally he discovered the right one. It's the same thing in your life; if you want to achieve something good, it takes time. If you failed at something a hundred times, how would you feel? Most likely you would feel totally discouraged. Yet, Edison didn't think about it that way. When asked about his unsuccessful attempts to create a light bulb, his response was always that he hadn't failed; he just had discovered a lot of ways to not make a light bulb. His attitude was "I'm closer each time," and because of that we all benefited.

My father always told us to never give up until we reached our goal. Often, instead of digging for water in one place deep down, we dig a little here, no water, so a little somewhere else, no water, and we keep moving around but never reach water. Or, let's say you're planning to make a table and you need to find the right tree for the wood. Once you find it, if you take one swing with an ax into the tree, it doesn't make a dent at first. You could think, "Well, I tried to cut down this tree, but it didn't work out," and then maybe you go try another tree or give up altogether. But you might choose to think, "OK, I did what I could today, and tomorrow I'll hit in the same place." For a while you can't see a change. However, once you have a dent, then you know where to hit. After you've gone half way, the tree will fall with its own weight.

When we start something, it's good to see it through to the end. After all, it might be interesting to see how it turns out. But so often when we begin something new, we give up too easily. If we lack focus and determination, then it's like we're just hitting or digging once here, then once there, then once someplace else, and getting discouraged when we don't see the desired result.

It is the same with Peace Breathing practice. As you practice breathing and thinking peace for yourself and others, you build determination and an "I'm closer each time" attitude. You also develop the desire to encourage others as much as you can in making a harmonious life. When we're out of harmony, the best way to get back is through love. Peace Breathing is a way to help you experience the true meaning of love.

Understanding this is one thing, but practicing it is something else. Be patient. Look at your life more deeply and be more mature. Do your best every day with whatever your situation is. When you're struggling with something or facing difficulties, know that once you get through it, you'll be that much stronger. So, have patience with yourself, always thinking you're moving forward, getting closer each time.

9 ◉ the foundation comes first

Driving down a well-kept street, we admire a beautifully constructed home. Walking in the woods, we fall in love with a particular type of flowering bush. Listening to a renowned poet, we become entranced by the words we hear. Watching a great sports performance we think, "Wouldn't it be great to be part of the winning team?" Hearing an articulate public speaker, we wonder what it would be like to be famous, brilliant and popular.

When I was growing up in Korea, every student dreamed of being captain of his or her classroom. It was considered a great honor. One of my junior high school teachers shared a story about his school days. When he was in grammar school, he was named the captain of his classroom. As such he enjoyed privileges, had a certain power over his classmates and was looked to as a role model. One day a fire broke out in his school. Panicked, he ran out as fast as he could. Once he reached a place of safety, it dawned on him that he should have made sure his classmates made it out too. Later he learned that a quiet, small, unpopular student stayed behind until the last minute and assisted those who needed help exiting the building. Stunned and ashamed, the captain used this humbling experience as a turning point in his life. He realized that a position alone did not make him a leader, and he began focusing on developing his own character rather than simply enjoying the perks of his position.

It is easy to casually think that we want certain things we have seen, to wish we were like certain people, or to desire a special position or rank. We may quickly judge people and events by their outward appearance, but appearances are only one part of the whole picture.

A beautiful home is much more than the outward face of the building. We might quickly be able to put up a facade that looks like the admired home, but without a strong foundation and careful construction it will never last. Like a house of cards, it will fall at the first movement of the wind. We might like a flowering bush so much that we decide to transplant it into our own yard. But if we carelessly focus only on pulling out the part of the bush we can see, we may end up destroying the root system and be left with a plant that has no chance of survival. If we try to write poetry without putting in our sincere effort, the words will be hollow and will not touch the hearts of others. If we become part of a great sports team without training and experience, we will never measure up to the achievements of the rest, and we will diminish the effectiveness of the entire team. If we gain a position of leadership but lack the background and confidence needed to sustain us, we will be incapable of leading when the time comes.

In all facets of life, time and patience are needed in order to build a strong foundation. The larger the building, the longer it takes to build its foundation. And yet, once the building is up and construction is complete, the foundation itself is invisible to us. We cannot measure the strength of a building simply by its external appearance. With the passing of time or when extreme forces are placed upon the building, the true strength of the foundation will reveal itself.

What is the foundation of our own lives? Are we drawn to power, glamour, or fame? Or are we working on building the positive characteristics we possess within? Somehow the quiet, unpopular student had built a stable foundation within himself so that he remained calm and had the courage to help others in a time of crisis. The popular captain, while in the position of leadership, was overwhelmed by the fire and thought of his own safety first. No matter what our experience has been up until now, we can learn from these examples. By enhancing our positive characteristics we will steadily create a lasting foundation built upon harmony. With time and patience, our strength of character will quietly and naturally shine through.

10 ● reflections on water

There are remote areas of our planet that go through a long and hot dry season each year. The Earth becomes parched, the riverbeds dry, the landscape barren. A quick rainstorm does not have much effect as the water runs over the hard ground and quickly evaporates. But when the rainy season finally arrives, the ground becomes saturated with the steady rainfall. Soon the riverbeds flow with water, and great pools begin to cover dry land. Plant life begins to thrive. Birds, animals and insects are drawn to these waterways, and fish somehow find their way into this fresh water system. The seemingly lifeless desert is now teeming with life.

Water quietly supports the existence of all life on Earth. Water naturally flows and follows the contour of the land. It cleanses and purifies. But its benefit to physical life is not the only thing that attracts us to water. We feel at peace when we walk near a beautiful secluded lake, exhilarated when we wade in a cold mountain stream and soothed when we listen to the rhythm of the ocean's waves. Water can provide us with a profound sense of harmony as we feel a connection with something greater than ourselves.

Sometimes we feel as if our lives have become parched and dry. We go through the motions of day-to-day activities without feeling that spark of life. We feel drained, unsatisfied and perhaps cynical. In times like these it is important for us to move toward that which awakens harmony within us, to regain our balance and rediscover how precious life is. While inner harmony may seem a distant dream, it continuously flows deep within the mind as it connects us to the greater harmony that we witness in nature and that flows throughout the universe.

We can begin moving toward harmony at this very moment. Our first step is breathing itself, as essential to life as water. As we take slow, deep breaths we begin to shed some of the tension we have been holding in our minds and bodies. Next, we need to turn our thoughts toward qualities that lead to a fulfilled life: harmony, joy, peace, contentment, love and gratitude. If we make an effort to breathe deeply and bring life-affirming thoughts to mind on a regular basis each day, we will eventually become saturated with harmony just like the parched Earth during the rainy season.

Peace Breathing can do this for us. It brings us closer to our deeper selves. By incorporating methods such as Peace Breathing into each and every day and patiently giving ourselves time to grow, our vibrant life naturally emerges. Through steady practice, just like the steady rainfall of the rainy season, we become saturated with the energy of peace and harmony, revitalizing ourselves and our surroundings. We create an environment where everything can grow and flourish. Then, just like the flowing water, our own happiness expands and, in turn, people are drawn to our peaceful nature.

11 ◉ the best recipe

For most of us, it's hard to resist a homemade chocolate chip cookie. Without getting into the calorie count or fat content here, it's safe to say that we simply enjoy the taste. If we're lucky, we may have a nice friend who brings us a fresh batch of our favorite cookies every time he or she bakes. But even our best friends don't always know when we happen to have a craving for those delicious chocolate chips.

If we have the recipe, we can enjoy the cookies whenever we want—if we take the time to bake them, that is. Even if we have a recipe for the ultimate chocolate chip cookie, some of us would put it aside until it eventually began gathering dust, while others would jump at the chance to whip up a batch right away. Those who let the recipe sit would rely on friends to occasionally bring them some cookies, having no choice as to when they can enjoy them. Those who decide to give it a try would be able to satisfy their sweet tooth more quickly and more often.

The first time we try the recipe though, the results may not come out as we expected. Maybe we forgot one ingredient or baked the cookies too long or had the oven at the wrong temperature. At this point some people would give up on baking altogether, calling themselves hopeless or perhaps blaming the recipe or the person who gave it to them. Others among us would learn from their mistakes and try to do better next time. After several attempts, we would finally taste the same wonderful cookies that our friend used to bake for us. We can then follow the same steps again and again. But in time, a few of us might start looking for something more. We begin tinkering with the recipe, adding a bit more of this or that in order to make the cookies even more delicious. With a little creativity and experimentation, the "best" chocolate chip cookies become even better, and soon our creation becomes the most requested recipe.

In life, we often think about the fact that we want to be happy or enjoy peace of mind. If we depend on others to provide these things for us, we are setting ourselves up for disappointment. No one else understands us and our lives like we do. It would be impossible for someone else to make us 100 percent happy or calm. Yet many people live this way, experiencing frequent highs and lows as they expect someone or something else to make them happy—to provide them with an endless supply of chocolate chip cookies.

Some of us realize that we must search within ourselves to attain happiness and harmony, and we have learned some type of method to help us attain these goals. But knowledge alone is not the deciding factor. Here again, there are those who actually practice the method consistently while others simply set it aside. They may brag about the fact that they have the best recipe, but in daily life they are simply allowing it to gather dust. Those who not only have the recipe but also follow it have a much better chance of finding what they are looking for.

Our first attempt to make improvements may not seem successful, just like our first batch of cookies. Some people become frustrated and give up immediately, calling themselves a failure or perhaps complaining that the method doesn't work or even becoming angry at the person from whom they learned it. Others see the experience as something to learn from, and they try the method again. It is, of course, the latter group that continues to move forward and grow. With patience and practice, these people get the most out of the method and eventually begin to get positive results. Finally, they can even find ways to enhance and improve the method they are practicing, truly making it their own.

People are naturally drawn to those who have a positive way about them, those who are truly happy and living in a harmonious way. There is no need for such people to shout, "I have the best recipe!" since others easily recognize the positive results they have achieved and are eager to learn their secret. Once we have found our own happiness, it becomes natural for us to want to share our experience with others. As we do, our own happiness grows as we help others to move in the direction of harmony in their own lives. Our energy expands as we pass on our recipe, helping others learn how to follow it, master it and then make improvements upon it in their own way.

If you're hungry for a chocolate chip cookie right now, that's understandable. If you're hungry for a sense of harmony and peace within, think about the recipe you may already know, and think about how you can put it into practice. There is no time like the present to begin your baking adventure.

12 ◉ accepting the unexpected

No matter how well we plan our lives or how organized we are, unexpected things can happen that change the end result. Even the most detail-oriented person has to make adjustments when, for some reason, everything does not go exactly as planned. There are times when any amount of planning would not have made a difference. For instance, we may spend weeks looking forward to meeting someone we admire, but on that day we get caught in a traffic jam and we cannot make the appointment. We may work hard on an important business presentation only to become ill on the day of the meeting. We may schedule a much needed vacation, but have to cancel due to a sudden family emergency.

Thorough planning only takes us so far. We must also be ready for the unexpected, to let go of our plans when an unforeseen situation presents itself. Some people try to strategize and think of every possible outcome. But planning to the point of obsession is counter-productive. It does us a disservice to spend all of our time and energy thinking about every possible situation that might come up.

First of all, there is always going to be something that we had not considered or that we can't control. And, it is often the extremely detail-minded person who becomes the most stressed when something unexpected happens. A more comfortable way to live would be first to do our best in any given situation and to then work on how we react when things do not go as planned.

Our response to unexpected change is a reflection of our mind's perspective. If we are accustomed to focusing only on our own wishes, needs and desires, we see the situation from a limited viewpoint with little room for adjustment. Without even realizing it, this perspective creates a rigid boundary around us, shrinking our energy and weighing us down. We become inflexible and demanding. Those who live with a bigger perspective have a way of accommodating new or unexpected circumstances in a natural way. As our boundaries crumble, we have more room within us to accept any situation as it comes without feeling upset or anxious. We find a way to get the most out of any experience and to learn from it as well.

Bright energy expands. With each new experience we build a stronger foundation for the next occurrence. But it is important to remember that this is a step-by-step process and that growth does not occur in one day. Patience will keep us moving in the right direction. Having patience with ourselves is not easy for many of us, but we must learn to love ourselves and to care about ourselves with as much compassion as we have toward our most precious loved ones. Through this process we begin to experience the way that harmony is created. Our mind becomes open.

We are more relaxed. We are able to see situations more clearly. We are able to accommodate the unexpected. People begin to notice that we have become calmer and easier to get along with. We enjoy being with people much more so than before. Our life becomes happier and more fulfilling. We appreciate all that we have and desire to continue evolving. We look forward to each new day.

13 ◉ the island

You need to visit a particular small island. You are able to borrow a boat, but are not familiar with the area and would like to have some help to find the island. The owner of a larger boat is going that way and agrees to lead you. To make life easier for yourself, you get the bright idea of tying your boat to his so you can just go along for the ride. You spend your time enjoying the sun, having drinks and snacks at your leisure, listening to music and turning the trip into a party.

Suddenly you notice that you're passing the island you wanted to reach, and the boat in the lead has continued moving toward its own destination. You rush to untie the heavy knot in the rope connecting your boat to his, but because it is so tight and has gotten wet and dirty, you can't get the knot undone. You are pulled past the island and are stuck going along with the larger boat, moving farther and farther away from where you want to be. You're angry and blame the large boat's owner for your problem. You finally get the knot untied but because you were so busy partying and then panicking, you're not sure how to get back to the island. You also discover that you're not familiar with operating your boat and have trouble with the controls. You end up drifting toward shore, somewhere between the island far behind you and the large boat which by now is out of sight.

People have a tendency to rely on someone else to get them where they want to go. We can be quick to give up our responsibility and let others drive our lives, and then blame them when things go wrong. We may feel like we've gotten the best of someone else by letting them do the work. But in the end it is rare that we find what we are looking for this way. This doesn't mean that we should live a solitary life and find our own way in everything we do. Rather, we need to be open to the assistance of others who may have more experience, and then take responsibility to get ourselves where we want to go. We can learn from others and benefit from their insights, but ultimately our own actions will lead us to our destination.

So let's start our story again. To reach the island in this scenario, you ask for assistance from the owner of the larger boat and if you can follow him toward the island. Any issues you have with operating the boat are apparent from the start, and you work them out before leaving. You pay attention to where you are going as you travel along the waterway. You carefully watch for the island and have no problem making the turn to reach your destination. Not only have you arrived at your destination, your journey to get there was smooth, and it has prepared you for future trips with the knowledge that you have learned along the way.

14 ◉ you're the driver

In each moment, we interact with the multitude of objects that exist all around us: buildings, trees, books, phones and so on. We may rarely think twice about the existence of our physical surroundings or even our own physical bodies. But those who have studied physics know that the physical world is much different than what it appears to be.

All material things—those that are alive and those that we consider to not be alive—are made up of atoms which are constantly in motion. Based upon scientific theory, if we break down each component of an atom to its smallest characteristic, the end result is a wave vibration. In other words, everything around us consists of waves. From this point of view, the physical world is much less solid and static than we usually think. We are composed of vibrations and interact with a world that is also composed of vibrations.

Our thoughts also consist of waves. Psychologists generally agree that our conscious mind is only a very small portion of our total mental capacity. Within our vast subconscious mind, we have recorded our thoughts, feelings, actions and all that we have observed. The energy within our subconscious mind has a direct impact on our daily lives, both mentally and physically. When enough of a certain type of energy is built up in the subconscious mind, we no longer have to think consciously about it. At a certain point, the influence of that energy moves us without any conscious thought on our part.

For example, when you drive to the store are you thinking to yourself: *Put the car in drive, step on the gas pedal with this much pressure, look left, look right, check the mirror, proceed at this speed, slow down by applying the brake at this rate, make a right turn at this angle and resume speed?* In all likelihood you are thinking about something totally unrelated to driving—what it is you want to buy at the store, what you have to do after shopping, plans for the weekend, your job, homework, or countless other subjects. Somehow your body goes through the motions of driving seemingly on its own. Why? Because you practiced the skill of driving over and over until it became a solid recording in your subconscious mind. From that point on you were able to drive based on the energy accumulated, thus you no longer needed to give the mechanics of driving your conscious attention.

We will never be capable of driving a car if we quit after our first attempt. It takes time before driving becomes natural to us. The same holds true for the concept of peace. We cannot expect peace to be part of our lives if we think about it momentarily only once in a while. We must build up the energy of peace and harmony into our minds on a regular basis. We must practice steering ourselves toward peaceful energy every day. Only then will peace and happiness become part of our daily lives, part of who we are, without us having to consciously think about it. When this happens, thinking of peace for ourselves and peace for others becomes as natural as driving a car.

15 ◉ practice, practice, practice

It takes time to achieve peace. Where the Mississippi River begins in Minnesota, the water is only knee deep. But the farther it flows, the wider and deeper it becomes. It's the same way with our practice: we need to take our time building up our energy step by step, continuously, so it can expand and deepen, just like the Mississippi.

You can start with sitting meditation in the morning for a length of time that is comfortable for you. Close your eyes. Breathe slowly and deeply. As you inhale, think "World." As you exhale, think "Peace."

Peace Breathing is also Moving Meditation. You can practice Peace Breathing anytime, anywhere. By practicing throughout the day—while you're walking, driving, working, eating—even though your energy may drop a little bit, you're consistently bringing it back up. You are able to maintain a more stable life.

It is better to change slowly over time. When you do a little here and a little there throughout the day, it adds up. Rather than think, "OK! Today I'm going to meditate 24 hours straight," try 5 minutes today, 5 minutes tomorrow, so then on the third day you wake up with 10 minutes more than before. When you start building positive energy, it doesn't seem to progress quickly. In the beginning, there is almost no difference between those who practice and those who don't. Then, at a certain point, those who practice will see their energy increase rapidly.

Continue your daily practice, no matter what. Inhale thinking "World" and exhale thinking "Peace." If you're happy or excited…if you're tired or depressed…if your favorite sports team wins or loses…if you're sick…if things are going well. No matter the situation: inhale World, exhale Peace.

If things are going well, you may think you don't need to practice Peace Breathing. But this is not the case. This is actually a good time to elevate your energy even more rapidly, if you use the opportunity wisely, because the positive impact of your practice is much greater. Whether things are stressful or things are going smoothly, please just practice consistently, sincerely and seriously. Instead of analyzing or worrying about your progress, just keep practicing World Peace.

You might think, "I don't have time for Peace Breathing," but when you don't practice, your energy becomes small and tight. Every little thing bothers you, and you can't get much of anything done. Instead of struggling with the situation, worrying, complaining or losing sleep, use that time to Peace Breathe. When you practice expanding your energy steadily, then you become less susceptible to what's going on around you. You are less impacted by distractions or other issues. Like the mighty Mississippi, your energy expands and deepens and continues to flow smoothly.

Peace Breathing is not simply something you practice because you need help or you want to make your own life better. Yes, it is for that, but it's also much bigger. It's to help Earth's progress. The beauty of thinking World Peace is that while you are growing, you are also benefiting humanity and all life on Earth. So, what do we need to do? Practice, practice, practice.

16 ● a balanced life

Picture a small round plate balanced on top of a chopstick. If anything is placed on the plate, it needs to be centered so the plate doesn't tip. Now magnify that picture until you can imagine yourself standing on top of the plate. You would need to stay in the center in order for the plate to stay balanced and for you to remain safely on top.

This kind of image makes balance easy to understand. But when we are looking for balance in our lives, we have a tendency to do the exact opposite of what it takes to stay in balance. We go to extremes. We disrupt our normal routine, squeeze in too many activities or maybe drop something meaningful, make abrupt changes or chase after the latest trend. It's as if we're on top of the plate and running one direction and then another and then another, constantly in motion and continuously off balance as the plate tips this way and that. Our energy is drained because so much of our time and effort is spent trying to regain our balance, yet it is our own actions that create the instability in the first place.

Think about when you are trying to make a decision and you keep going back and forth in your mind. You might be up half the night thinking, "Yes, no, yes, no," and in the morning you wake up with a headache instead of a clear answer. No matter what you decide, it is likely that you will second-guess yourself as the mind continues to shift. It is as if your mind is racing from one side of the plate to the other, off balance and never finding resolution. You become exhausted and discouraged. Even if you made the best possible decision, your self-doubt and worry prevent you from fully benefiting.

What if we could stay in the center of the plate? From the center, everything is visible and we can see all directions equally. The plate becomes a stable surface. Our energy is gathered together rather than scattered in many directions. But even here, we may still worry about tipping one way or another if we somehow move off of the center. There is one more aspect that needs to be improved. What if the chopstick holding the plate becomes a massive column, perhaps even as wide as the plate? Now our foundation is completely secure and, even if we do move one direction or another, we are not wasting one bit of energy trying to regain our stability. We can walk around the whole plate without losing our balance.

How do we get ourselves to the center? How do we enlarge the column? The answer to both questions is the same. We need to open our mind and expand its energy. Think about how you feel when you are truly happy or experience a deep sense of peace. You feel at ease, light as a feather, accommodating and full of possibilities. This is an example of expanded energy. But when you are upset, angry or worried, you feel tight and constricted. Your mood is dark. Your reaction to things can be unpleasant. When we haven't experienced expansive energy over a long period of time, even the tiniest things bother us.

Here's another way to look at it: if you have a small bowl of water and drop a large rock into it, the water splashes everywhere and the bowl is broken into pieces. You've lost the water and the bowl, and you are devastated. But if the same rock is dropped into the middle of Lake Michigan, you will only notice a few bubbles as it slips into the water. The lake is so big that any impact made by the rock, in comparison to the size of the lake, is nearly unnoticeable. Ideally, we'd like our mind to be as big as Lake Michigan instead of as small as the bowl. Then even if something happens that might have been devastating, we recover almost instantly. We are able to absorb the impact, and it disappears almost as quickly as it appeared, like a bubble.

My father had an experience that illustrates both the physical and energy aspects of balance. Back in Korea, he had branches of his educational organization all over the country. During a trip to one of his school locations on a remote island off the coast, he was riding in a small boat with other passengers when high waves came up. The boat began to rock violently. Nearly everyone on the boat started to shout and cry in panic. Some of them stood up and tried to move around the boat. The captain of the boat was unable to restore order. My father loudly ordered everyone to sit down and be quiet. Everyone immediately followed his command. Although the ride was rough, the boat made it safely to shore. Without everyone staying in their seats, the boat would have literally lost its balance and everyone would have been thrown into the dangerous waters. With my father's strong balanced energy, he knew in an instant what had to be done to stay safe. And because of the power of his balanced energy, my father spoke with confidence and authority, so that every person on the boat listened to him and reacted instantaneously.

Balanced energy is something that can be attained through Peace Breathing. With consistent practice you will create more and more bright, expansive energy with each breath. Gradually you will start to enjoy life and find that problems and challenges don't throw you off like they used to. Peace Breathing helps us move toward the center where we find stability and can see everything clearly. It also helps us build a larger foundation so that our lives are firmly supported by the immense power of harmony and peace. With your newly expanded energy, you are no longer filled with doubt. If you make a mistake you learn from it instead of draining your energy by criticizing yourself. Relationships are smoother, and day-to-day life is more balanced. And when the time comes, your deeper wisdom and self-confidence spontaneously surface. You will find that you can face major sudden challenges calmly and decisively, without a trace of wavering within your mind. The true energy of peace—strong, steady, calm—will guide you to a more harmonious and balanced life.

17 ● making a genuine connection

Unlike any time before in Earth's history, the 21st century is, and will continue to be, a time of tremendous change. We already see great changes in political and economic situations. We see vast changes in the Earth's environment. We feel huge changes in the pace and energy of our daily lives. Whether we know it or not, whether we pay attention to it or not, these dramatic changes are taking place to move us forward, to bring us closer to the energy within the universe—the energy of great harmony. The renewal of the universe continues to move forward in this direction. The question is: How ready are we for these changes?

Human beings play an important role as to how the energy of the universe is used and expressed on Earth. In this sense, we are all joined as members of Earth's family, and we all share the responsibility for our planet's future. Our collective energy determines the Earth's future. In times of rapid change, we often forget what we need to do. Yet even in the midst of all these changes, we can navigate in a smooth way by tuning in to the harmony of the universe.

To illustrate this concept, let's say we have an excellent sound system with a powerful amplifier and the most sensitive speakers available. If we connect the two with high quality speaker wire, we will enjoy the beautiful, pure sound that was originally generated. But even with the best components, the sound can become distorted and weak if the speaker wire is full of impurities. We may blame the amplifier or perhaps the speakers, but it is the wire itself causing the problem. Even with a wireless connection, we can still have distortions if there is interference in the signal. A solid, genuine connection must exist for the true sound to be realized.

How we use the flow of energy from the universe is similar to this speaker wire example. Our thoughts, words and actions can either facilitate the flow of harmonious energy to our planet or distort it with impurities. If our thoughts, words and actions are directed toward harmony, the beautiful energy of the universe will flow to us smoothly and naturally, and a world of peace and harmony will eventually be revealed. On the other hand, non-positive thoughts, words and actions cause disturbances in the flow of the universe's energy, and a world far from harmony is the result. We must remember that the harmonious energy of the universe is always present and always flowing. Only when we are tuned in to that pure energy and are allowing it to flow will we see the positive results in our lives and on our planet.

Our planet will continue to see tremendous change in this century. The question is: Will it be for the better or for the worse? The answer: It is up to us. We must take responsibility each day, each moment, for our own thoughts, words and actions because they directly contribute to the collective energy of Earth. When our minds are bright and peaceful, when our attitudes are sincere, when our words are kind and encouraging, when our actions arise from consideration of others, we are fully living in harmony with the vast energy of the universe. We are all part of Earth's family. We must always remember our collective energy determines the Earth's future.

18 ◉ doing the dishes

When it comes time to wash the dishes, we need water. It also helps if some soap is available to do the job right. But even with the best soap and plenty of scrubbing, the dishes won't really be clean until they are thoroughly rinsed. If we think we're done with the dinner dishes after scrubbing them with soap and water, we'll discover a bigger mess in the morning as the soap residue dries up and hardens.

We may have a desire to improve ourselves, to eliminate our non-positive habits and characteristics, that is, to clean up our messy dishes. Making a decision to improve is the first step, the same as deciding to do the dishes in the first place. This in itself is an important step. Over time, those who have no interest in bettering themselves may become more and more like a kitchen where the dishes have not been done for months. Just as soap makes the dishwashing easier, having an effective method to improve ourselves will help us accomplish our goals that much faster. We may still eventually reach our goal without a specific process, just as we could wash the dishes without soap, but having a system in place makes the job that much easier.

Once we have found a method, it will be of no use to us unless we apply it to our lives. We may think that we understand the theory behind a method and complain that it has not helped us reach our goal, but if we haven't actually tried to put it into action, it is as if we've washed the dishes without rinsing them. Following through to the next step is essential. Only by putting the process into practice will we begin to see the results, to form new habits and enhance our more positive characteristics.

For most of us, it has become natural to go through the steps of washing the dishes each day and having clean dishes to use the next time around. The same type of approach applies to the practice of Peace Breathing or any other effective method of self-improvement. Daily effort must be made if we wish to have consistent results. Initially, just as with a large pile of dirty dishes, it may feel like an overwhelming task. But as we work on it, one by one, step by step, eventually we will see progress. And the closer we get to our goal, the better we will feel and the more motivated we will become to continue to take more steps forward. Then, with each improvement we make, we become ready for the next level of improvement to come. Over time our Peace Breathing or other positive habit becomes as natural to us as doing the dishes every day.

19 ● healing our planet

Whether we live in a place surrounded by forests and mountains or in an urban area where we catch a glimpse of the sky every now and then, nature is something that can bring comfort and serenity to us all. Just seeing the sun shine or hearing the wind in the trees can help us to take a step back from the demands of daily life. We feel refreshed when we take a deep breath of fresh air or listen to the sound of the waves. We come alive when we see a lush garden or spot a mother duck leading her row of ducklings to water.

Nature gives us many lessons, including the examples of selfless giving and living life to the fullest. The sun provides its energy equally to all and asks nothing in return. A plant finds a way to grow whether it is in fertile soil or lodged between the cracks of the sidewalk. Moment by moment, nature continuously pours forth its life energy, and we benefit in countless ways.

The Gaia theory views Earth as an interconnected, living entity, with all life forms and all of nature playing integral and supportive roles to ensure survival. Unfortunately this living system has suffered due to many careless actions of human beings. We tend to see this as a problem of government policies or business and industry. What we may not realize is that each and every human being plays an important role in the healing of our planet.

Because nature does not "speak" according to our way of thinking, it is a rare person who even considers communicating with nature. Common knowledge tells us that rocks are lifeless, and while plants are alive, their lives are completely different and separate from the lives of human beings. But the concepts we believe today will change, and need to change, as individuals and society continue to evolve. For example, there was a time in history when it was common knowledge that the Earth was flat and it was unacceptable to believe otherwise. Our knowledge has increased and evolved. Ideas considered foolish in the past are proven facts today.

Taking this into account, how do we really know that all of our surroundings—from air to water to soil to rocks—are not alive? If we can think of life in terms of energy, we can see the commonality among all existences on earth. Rocks seem lifeless, but in reality they cannot form without energy. If something has energy, then it has life. There is a harmony and balance that binds together the protons, neutrons and electrons of each atom and creates the basis for all life. There is also a harmony and balance that is inherent in nature but that human beings have disrupted over a long period of time.

Our thoughts, too, consist of energy, and thoughts of harmony and care have a healing effect on us as well as on our surroundings. As we send love and respect to nature, we feel the benefit of this. At the same time, we expand our vision and begin to recognize our deep connection with all of nature. We gain much from being out in nature, but nature needs us to be respectful and to consider it as our companion.

Nature is continually giving. We can enjoy nature and benefit from its energy, but we must give back to it too. This is not merely a kind thing to do, but it is necessary for our survival. To always take and never give is not sustainable. The Earth's natural resources must be protected. If we recognize this and bring it into our thoughts on a daily basis, we will naturally communicate love and respect to nature.

Our thoughts, words and actions create energy that impacts nature. If we strive to make every thought a thought of harmony, every action an action of gratitude, and every breath a breath of peace, we become a precious and invaluable part of the Earth's healing process.

20 ◉ finding your way

Like most first-time visitors to Chicago, you want to see the city's tallest building, Willis Tower (formerly called Sears Tower). As you drive into the city, it is easy to spot. Willis Tower naturally stands out from all of the other buildings because of its massive size and distinct shape. But as you head in that direction, at some point the Tower is no longer in view because you are suddenly surrounded by other tall buildings.

Not being familiar with Chicago and without GPS, you may take a guess at the direction but can easily become confused and go the wrong way. If you go far enough in the wrong direction, you will suddenly see that the Tower is behind you and realize your mistake. So you turn around and try again. You even ask for directions this time, but because you are unfamiliar with the streets, you find the directions hard to follow. When you move back into the downtown area with its many tall buildings, you get confused and make another wrong turn. You realize your mistake more quickly this time and finally find yourself moving closer to your destination. When you ask for directions again, you find they are easy to follow because you are so close. The next thing you know, you are right in front of Willis Tower.

When we practice Peace Breathing, we will experience a similar pattern of getting closer to and further away from our goal or destination. Even if we desire to get to our goal as directly and quickly as possible, we can easily get distracted by events and situations, large or small. It is important that we take the first step of setting up a clear goal. Then, we need to be persistent and not give up because we have made a mistake. In fact, we can learn from our mistakes.

If we become temporarily side-tracked, we need to turn back in the right direction. Maintaining our focus requires patience and steady practice. As we get closer and closer to our destination, it may feel as if it is becoming harder to reach. We'll think we still have a long way to go. But if we keep pushing toward our goal, before we know it, we'll find that we are there.

21 ● above and below

When the sky is full of clouds, even if it is raining below, the sun is still shining above. Most people take this to mean that when it rains, we need to keep our mind above the clouds where the sun is shining. But actually we need to consider both the bright sun above and the darkness below.

People tend to associate rainy days with gloominess. But the right amount of rain is essential to sustain all life on Earth. If the sun was always shining, Earth would become a desert. If it was always raining, the Earth would flood. Even though the sky is dark and we may become cold and soaked, we need to understand the importance of rain. Without this vital natural resource, we would have no drinking water, no trees, no grass and no animals. Even the ground itself could not survive, and eventually all life would disappear. Rainy days are a vital part of life. Although the experience of being soaking wet may be uncomfortable, it is necessary for all life.

We need to see the benefits of rain and feel gratitude for it while, at the same time, know that rain storms do not last forever. During a storm the sun is still definitely shining above, and when the clouds pass by, the sun will shine on us again. The energy of the sun above the clouds and of the rain below the clouds is needed for life to continue and to flourish.

In daily life, we tend to feel a constant mix of moods. We need to remind ourselves that deep within us, we are consistently pure and bright just like the constantly shining sun. This can help us avoid being pulled down into gloominess. The challenging times we go through are part of our own evolution, just as rain and sun are part of Earth's evolution.

When you are faced with a situation that you feel is undesirable and uncomfortable, know that it will not last forever. Try to accept the situation as it is without complaints or other negative energy. And, if possible, go one step further and try to feel gratitude. Understand that you will become wiser through every experience. You may understand why some things occur, but even if you don't, you may still learn something. Bring to mind your deeper self, the self who is full of harmony.

Just as rain is necessary for nature and the Earth's progress, all your experiences are necessary for your growth. Face every situation and see each as part of your own life's growth as well as part of the greater process of clearing out old non-positive energy for yourself and the world. Know that every experience you have will make you stronger and better prepared for the next rainy day. With this perspective you are taking the deeper view by simultaneously looking above and below the clouds.

22 ● the bridge to your future

Many types of bridges exist. Some are merely functional—they do their job but are not much to look at. A small stone bridge over a stream may be quite simple, yet eye-pleasing and enjoyable. Others are made for foot traffic only, perhaps artistically crafted, perhaps unexceptional. And some bridges are architectural wonders, amazing in their ability to span large bodies of water or to support massive highways or railways. What they all have in common is the function of helping people get to where they want to go.

If you live in a secluded area and can see land on the other side of a river, you may think about what it might be like over there. But if you're never able to cross the river, you will never know what it's like. In the same way that you might imagine what it's like on the other side of the river, it is important to look into your own future and think about the possibilities that exist. Although you don't have a complete picture of your future, you need to think about your bigger, long-term goals so that you can take steps now to move in that direction.

We can apply this idea of building bridges in our lives. On the most basic level, we first need to consider our starting and ending points. Will our materials be strong enough to support our bridge? Where would we like to go? Building our own bridges takes place in day-to-day life. When we face small challenges, do we stop right there and try to avoid the situation? Do we rely on someone else to resolve the problem? Do we blame others, complain, or make excuses instead of trying to find a solution? Or do we utilize our previous experience and creativity to find a way to work it out?

The manner in which we deal with the small things in daily life creates the foundation for our ability to cope with bigger and more complicated challenges that may come in our future. If we have not used our daily life to build the small, simple bridges, we may not be ready to build a larger and stronger one when we need it most. If we have always followed in someone else's footsteps and counted on others to create bridges for us, then we will not be able to easily build our own bridge. It may take a long time to figure out the best place to cross, the materials needed, and the method to build each bridge. Extensive trial and error will give further delay to our progress. We might even decide to stop right then, rather than make the effort, thus never knowing what lies ahead.

Those who have continuously built bridges in the direction of their goals are likely to be experts at bridge building. Their goals will become more focused and precise as they move closer to accomplishing them. If their vision encompasses a wide perspective, such as the desire to live with harmony and compassion, this too will be reflected in the bridges that they build. They will be able to accommodate others, like the huge bridges supporting highways and railways. Their bridges are also likely to be inspiring, unique and artistic. These people are easy to be around, generating sincere warmth and openness while lending quiet support to others who may need assistance in creating their own bridges.

Peace Breathing is a way for us to build a bridge to the future. When we work from a place of peace, the bridges we build are sturdy, accommodating and beautiful. Best of all, when our bridges are built, they lead us to a new, expansive life. We can see and experience things we've never seen or felt before. We are able to understand the connection between our old experiences and our new experiences. Our bridges open up new pathways for others to cross and explore each side of the land without limitations. Not only have we expanded our own energy, we have helped others to do the same. Thanks to the bridges we have built, we have created a new flow of energy, and the harmony we used to dream of is now reality.

23 ◉ the clean-up

Many people have the goal of keeping themselves on a positive track, trying to turn their lives toward harmony instead of falling into old negative habits. Yet the more we strive to build our positive side, the more we seem to notice all the non-positive things about ourselves. This is discouraging until we understand that this is actually part of our growth process.

Let's say we have a pond that hasn't been looked after for many years. We could leave the pond alone and try to forget about it, or we could see the pond's potential and begin the effort to clean it up. Our desire to make it better is a clear sign that we have bright energy within us initiating this change. This is our first big step in creating a positive environment for the future.

At first we are excited about the clean-up, but soon we seem to have a bigger mess than when we started. Some people give up at this point, letting the cleansing process discourage them and deciding to let the pond waste away, rather than do the work needed for its improvement. But those who move forward are taking the next major step toward a brighter future.

As we start the clean-up process, we find that the pond contains an old refrigerator, a couple of tires and a broken bicycle. Time and effort are needed to remove each of these large items from the pond, but the hard work is worth it because, once they are gone, our environment has improved dramatically. We start to see the pond's potential. Yet, the cleansing process doesn't stop here. We soon realize that many small items are also disturbing the beauty of our pond—a discarded shoe over here, a bottle and a can over there. So we have to remove each of these small items as well.

While we are knee-deep in the cleansing process, we notice more and more junk that has accumulated over time. It's easy to feel that other people's ponds are much better than ours. But we must remain focused on our own cleansing process. Instead of being discouraged by the clutter, we must continue to imagine how beautiful it will be when we are done. Others may simply be neglecting their ponds or trying to cover them up, and they will eventually have an even bigger mess to clean.

Once we have put in the time and effort to clean our pond, we feel great about the results. Nature begins to blossom around the pond, and we enjoy spending time there. Other people are drawn to its beauty and peacefulness.

We can relate the cleaning of our pond to the improvement of our mind. As our energy improves, we start seeing what we hadn't seen before. First we notice the big things weighing down our energy. Once we let go of the big things, we're able to see the small things and clean those things up too. The result is that our energy expands. We have more capacity to create something even greater, and we can more easily manage the little things as they come up. We see what we are capable of doing and how to move forward for the better. We see and remove the negative thoughts that linger in the corners of our mind. We know that our mind has become brighter, our vision clearer and our perspective wider. When the cleansing process of our mind is complete, we can see clearly to the depths of our own true existence.

24 ● oranges and apples

Let's say you live in an area where the only fruit available is an orange. It's the only kind of fruit you know about, so whenever you hear the word "fruit" you always think "orange." One day someone tells you about apples, but the description really means nothing to you. The person tells you, "An apple is also a fruit," but you say, "I don't think so. I've never seen one like that."

This person might go a step further and plant an apple tree for you, but that still doesn't help you to know what an apple is. You might ignore the tree and stick with your oranges, continuing to think that oranges are the only kind of fruit that exists. Or, if you are somewhat open, you might nurture the tree and see what happens.

However, it takes a long time for a tree to grow. If you are patient, you will find that the tree eventually bears fruit. But even then, you have to wait until fall arrives for the apples to ripen. If you pick the fruit too soon, you still won't have a clear understanding of an apple. If you wait until the apples are ripe, you might decide that you now know what an apple is because you have watched it grow and can see its completed shape and color. However, it is not until you pick the apple and taste it that you really understand what an apple is and come to the realization that there is more to fruit than just oranges.

Our options are very limited when we are set in our ways. Having fixed ideas makes it difficult to accommodate situations that are not "oranges." Often a person like this experiences greater suffering than they might otherwise because it is very hard for them to accept their surroundings, especially in a changing world. They are always looking for "orange" personalities, "orange" situations and "orange" solutions, when in fact an apple or a pear would be more fitting.

When someone tells you that an apple or a pear is also a fruit, would you say, "No, that's not a fruit. Goodbye," or would you have an open mind and ask, "May I have a piece?" If you choose to reject the idea of an apple or a pear as a fruit, you will never get to taste one. If you happen to be in a place that has no oranges, how would you feel? You'd be lost and anxious. Even if apples or pears were on your plate, you wouldn't know what to do with them. You wouldn't know that these are other options.

When we hold onto fixed, narrow viewpoints, it is not likely that we will find happiness. We limit our options and limit our enjoyment of life. If we can accept the possibility of other ideas and perspectives, we break down boundaries and live beyond our direct experiences. With this expanded energy we have a better chance of enjoying the fruits of a fulfilled life.

25 ● individuals impact the world

We do not live isolated lives. We are all part of one world. As such, it is important that we consider the impact of our individual lives on our families, neighbors, the society in which we live, and throughout the world. We can see how large global incidents can impact the individual, but we generally are not aware that the opposite is also true: each of us can impact the world. This is a concept we all must strive to understand and put into practice in a positive way.

This brings us to the topic of energy—energy we create through our thoughts, words and actions. For instance, we can easily see non-positive energy in rush hour traffic, when people cut in front of each other and honk their horns. How many of us have answered in the same way? Is this truly the type of energy we wish to create, to live in, and to send out? Wouldn't it be better to respond calmly? We surround ourselves with the type of energy with which we respond, whether it's positive or non-positive. We have to stop and make a conscious effort to contribute positive energy to a situation, ultimately building strong energy for ourselves and for the world.

Every day each one of us has a choice about the type of energy we wish to build. One person can change the energy of a situation for better or worse. Think of it this way: Suppose you have a lake with a number of streams that flow into the lake. Are the streams clean or contaminated? If even one stream is contaminated it will make the lake unclean, and contaminate the fish in the lake and pollute the water that people drink. The contamination from that one stream will impact many things. It's the same with us and how we think, speak and act in the world. We can be a positive influence or not. Even the little things we do—at home, at work, at school—all contribute to the energy we create collectively. The energy from our small bursts of anger and frustration adds to the conflicts taking place around us and throughout the world.

We can easily become overwhelmed thinking about the world's issues. Instead of worrying, let's use that time to think World Peace and express it in our lives. When you and I and others practice peace in this way, the collective energy of peace adds up and becomes a sizeable amount. Then something that once seemed impossible becomes possible. Problems that seemed unsolvable are approached from a new perspective. Previously unseen solutions come to light. This is the deeper meaning behind Peace Breathing: to contribute to the peace and harmony of all humanity through the daily practice of individuals.

26 ◉ washing your clothes

Why do you wash your clothes? To clean the dirt away, right? You know that the detergent will separate the dirt from the clothing. When you wear clean, freshly washed clothes you feel good and comfortable. But once you get your clothes cleaned, do you think, "Oh, I don't have to clean this anymore"? Of course not. You know that your clothes will get dirty and need to be washed again.

Keeping your clothes clean is a continual process, just like Peace Breathing. You have to practice consistently, not just wash your clothes once. Cleaning up for one day, 24 hours straight, does not work—for laundry or for your Peace Breathing practice.

Cleaning out negative energy through your practice is not always easy. It's a process of clearing out the old energy to make room for fresh energy. Most people don't make this effort. It requires some hard work and energy itself. You may recognize areas in your life that need to be improved, but you give up because it's too hard, or sometimes you feel lazy. You just don't want to do it, and so you continue to hold on to old energy.

And the cleaning process might not be comfortable. Part way through it, you can feel nervous and anxious, unsure of what's next. You may regret that you even started this process. You may wish to go back to where you started because even if it was not a great place to begin with, at least it was familiar. If you understand everything as a process of renewing, then you realize that each difficult situation you encounter is actually like a detergent meant to help scrub the dirt. After this happens you can wear fresh, clean energy.

Many people, however, rather than having the courage and determination to clean themselves up, would rather throw mud at others and say, "Ha ha ha! Look at how dirty they are." We've got to stop doing that. Instead of finding faults in others, we need to focus on ourselves and our own issues. We all have something in our lives that needs to be cleaned up and improved, such as our non-positive attitudes.

Clean clothes feel so good when we first put them on. We have a fresh feeling. That's what Peace Breathing does: every time we practice Peace Breathing, we feel good, just like we do when we put on clean clothes.

27 ◎ in harmony with the universe

What do the universe and the atom have in common? We call the universe infinite, its size and scope being beyond our imagination. We know of the Big Bang Theory, which explains to us that the universe continuously expands. We observe our own solar system, with planets rotating predictably around the sun, and moons around the planets. We think of our Milky Way Galaxy, a vast number of stars tied together in a beautiful rotating pattern, and of an infinite number of galaxies co-existing in the expansive universe.

On the other end of the spectrum we can look at a much smaller perspective—the perspective of the atom. At its center are a certain number of protons and neutrons, with a specific number of electrons orbiting the center.

So, what do the universe and the atom have in common? Harmony and balance. We witness harmony in the movement of the planets around the sun as well as in the electrons circling the atom's center. Without harmony and balanced energy, the universe could not exist. Our solar system, including Earth, would collapse, and atoms would lose their structure and characteristics.

Although Earth is just one small component of the universe, our planet is still part of its great harmony. Human beings are also part of this great harmony. If our energy is blocked or unbalanced, we lose the essence of who we are. The question for each of us is this: Are we connecting to the harmony of the universe and letting it flow naturally, or are we blocking it?

In essence, all human beings exist with a fundamental connection to harmony and balance, but we have created many obstacles to this inner nature in today's world. When we have a lot of internal conflict the mind is anxious and indecisive. We waste a lot of time and energy this way. When we cheat or hurt others we are bound to have an uneasy mind and a life filled with stress because these actions are far from our most basic harmony. When we disrespect or attempt to control others, they lose their respect for us and we become isolated. This is far from the harmony that exists deep within us.

We are part of the universe. It's easy to forget this connection because our lives are too busy. We need to remind ourselves that we are living as part of this great universe. We have to follow its principles in order to live balanced and harmonious lives. Everything stems from our own individual energy, created by our thinking and expressed in our words and actions. The key is to focus our minds in the direction of the harmony that exists within and around us and to remind ourselves of our connection to the great harmony of the universe.

28 ◈ a breakthrough

"Just keep Peace Breathing!" These words were often spoken by my father. After a lifetime of meditation and research, he taught us to inhale thinking "World" and exhale thinking "Peace" as a way to build peace for ourselves, our families, our communities, nations and the entire world. We can begin to sense the strength of this method when we think of the effect that drops of water have on their surroundings. A single drop of water appears to be insignificant when compared to a huge rock. Yet steady and focused dripping, one drop at a time, can cause a boulder to crack and even break apart.

With consistent and focused Peace Breathing practice, we can feel our non-positive characteristics losing power and eventually crumbling away. We also find that our sense of inner harmony increases ever so slightly, day by day, until at a certain point we realize that our lives have become happier and that a new level of inner peace has been achieved.

During the gradual process of making your life brighter, the key is to appreciate your life as it is now. Sometimes when my father heard people discussing their problems or concerns for the future, he would respond strongly, "Forget about it! Just keep practicing Peace Breathing!" He was very right. If you can appreciate the circumstances you are in right now regardless of what they are, that is very important. Otherwise you will waste a lot of energy without gaining anything positive in return. We have to remember that the tougher something is, the closer we are to having a breakthrough. Have gratitude for the situation you are in even if it is uncomfortable. If you resist or get upset, complain or are angry, you are hurting yourself and blocking the flow of energy to you.

Appreciation is bright energy. If your thoughts are bright and positive, you can see yourself and your situation more clearly. Building bright energy is more important than anything because it affects you and at the same time it impacts others. You build bright energy within yourself and at the same time send that same bright energy out. The more that you send out calm, harmonious energy, the more of the same energy comes back to you. It opens you to learn from every situation. You will gain wisdom and insight from every experience, good or bad, if you can appreciate that experience for what it is. This knowledge will help you to handle something similar the next time it comes up. If you don't learn from it, you will experience the same struggle over and over again.

You might wonder why you are in a certain situation or blame someone for making you unhappy, but you have to remember that it's your perspective that causes you to think that way. There's a reason behind why you meet someone. There's a reason for all the connections you've made. You may not know what those reasons are at the time, but later you may understand how the situation was an important part of your life's journey.

Practice with a pure, sincere childlike mind. Remember what you're here for: to learn to love yourself and love others. If you learn how to forgive yourself, you also will know how to forgive others. Let's keep Peace Breathing with the confidence that each breath is moving us one step closer to harmony and peace for ourselves and for the world.

29 ◎ painting a clear self-portrait

Each day of our lives we face numerous decisions. Many of them are so small we don't even realize that we are making them. We automatically rely on our experience and knowledge and act upon our decisions without thinking. If we consider this carefully, we realize that much of our daily life is determined by our past, by all the things we have stored in our subconscious. Some decisions are much larger, and we must consciously think about them. But even then, our conscious thoughts combine with our recorded knowledge and experience in order for us to arrive at a conclusion. We may wish to make better decisions, but how? The answer lies in how clearly we are able to see ourselves.

If we absorb every experience and idea without sorting out what is valuable to us and what is not, we end up with a hodgepodge of sometimes conflicting information that may lead to confusion. Without a clear idea of the kind of person we would like to be, it becomes very easy to be swayed this way and that by the countless experiences and ideas circling around us.

It's like painting a picture. With a clean canvas and ample art supplies, we have an opportunity to create something we like. But if we approach the project without a clear idea of what we wish to create, we may not be happy with the results. Soon after we begin painting, we may find ourselves trying to fix it here and change it there, and paint over what we've already done. As the painting becomes more muddled, we might decide to switch the whole concept. Finally, we have a mishmash of colors and shapes that even we can't figure out.

To avoid this problem, the first step is to define a goal, a vision of what we would like to make. People who have a general idea of what they'd like to create have a better chance of achieving it. At first the image might be unclear. That's OK. It takes time for it to come together and take shape. If we remain patient and stay focused, the image will eventually be brought to life. With a clear picture in mind, we can paint something beautiful.

In terms of your life, what would you like to create? What do you see as your self-portrait? We must take time to think about this until we formulate a clear idea of the kind of person we truly wish to be. This goes beyond a career path or hobby, but relates to the fundamental aspects of our character. If we are living aimlessly, feeling conflicted and confused, it is especially important for us to take this step of defining ourselves and our lives as we wish to be. Peace Breathing can help us with this.

Once we have visualized our self-portrait, we must hold fast to the goal we have set for ourselves and concentrate on creating that painting, pouring our thoughts and our energy into the image of what we wish to be. We need to keep our thoughts positive and bright, always believing that we will be able to accomplish our goal. Peace Breathing and other methods that work to build the positive energy in our minds will help us to stay on this course and continue moving forward.

With our Peace Breathing practice, the beautiful image of our self-portrait will eventually appear as we first had in mind—or perhaps even greater than we ever imagined. Happy painting!

30 ◉ embrace the energy of today

What did you think when you woke up this morning? *Just another day.* Or maybe, *I don't want to get up.* Who did you see when you looked in the mirror? *Same old me, same as any other day.* What did you feel when you walked out the door? *Same street, same routine.* It's easy to think that today will be just like any other day and that we are the same as we were yesterday.

But even in 24 hours changes take place within us. We might not see them, but they're happening. Cells, the foundation for the physical body's structure, are newly forming within our bodies all the time. Our skin, our internal organs, our blood are all changing and renewing. Our mind, too, is not the same as it was the day before. The nature of the mind is to expand. The nature of the body is to renew. Even as we get older, we may feel weaker or more tired because the pace of the body's renewal slows down, but still the body is renewing. Vital, vibrant energy flows within the body and mind.

Yet too often we hold on to yesterday's mood and yesterday's energy instead of welcoming this powerful new resource of today. Even if yesterday was the best day of our lives, today's energy is new and fresh in comparison.

As an example, if we pour clean water into a bowl, it will start out being fresh. Over the course of the day, though, it will gradually begin to stagnate. If we try to use the same water the following day, it will no longer be fresh. It is obvious to us that it is better to use the water when it is fresh than when it is stagnant.

However, we tend to have little awareness of how this applies to daily life. All too often we carry stagnant energy within our minds and bodies instead of tapping into the rejuvenating, fresh energy flowing within us and around us. Sometimes we carry stagnant energy from a long time ago that weighs us down and holds us back. Even though new energy continuously is created, it mixes with the stagnant energy we have held onto and diminishes the power of today's new energy.

It is difficult for the body to be healthy and the mind to be clear and open if we are living with energy from the past. Yet many people live their lives based on yesterday, on things that are already gone. It's not that we need to forget our old experiences entirely or that they aren't valuable. After all, they helped us to get where we are today. The key is to look at our old experiences with a new perspective that makes them come alive rather than with our old way of thinking.

If we could only freely accept the new energy of each day and leave behind the energy of yesterday, then we could live much more energetically, optimistically, and contentedly. If we let our energy flow, rather than allow it to stagnate, we see the new possibilities in each moment. The expansive nature of the mind combined with the renewal of our physical cells provides us with new life every single day. What a difference it makes to embrace this energy rather than to live in the shadow of yesterday.

So, as you wake up in the morning, leave the past behind by making your first thought one of joy, hope, gratitude, and renewal. Then through Peace Breathing continue to move within the flow of today's new life, moment by moment.

31 ◉ playing in harmony

Have you ever heard what it sounds like before a classical music concert when all of the musicians are warming up? Everyone is playing at once, but not together. No one seems to pay any attention to what others are playing around them. It sounds like noise, not music.

Once the concert begins, all of the musicians play together harmoniously. This means that sometimes, for example, the violins come in very strong and loud. At other times, it may be the percussion or the horns that become stronger for a while and then quiet again as the focus moves to other instruments. The musicians give it their all when it's their turn to play and then soften to allow others the opportunity to shine. This kind of give-and-take goes on throughout a concert. Whether one instrument is being featured or all of the musicians are playing together, they have to listen to each other so that each unique instrument blends with the whole in a balanced way to create the magical sound we call music.

The physical body acts like an orchestra. Think of all of its different parts. The brain is really active when we try to solve a problem. Our digestive system gets busy when we eat. Our legs work hard when we walk down the street. But no matter what part of the body seems to be working the hardest at any given moment, the reason it is able to work hard is that the rest of the body is quietly supporting it in the background.

We must orchestrate this same type of harmony in our own lives. Without harmonious thoughts, our energy becomes noisy and distracted. Nothing is clear. We can't make decisions. We can't take action. If we just think about ourselves and do whatever we want, and others do the same, our self-centered actions are just like noise. It is almost impossible to achieve anything meaningful this way. Instead we need to consider our actions in relation to others. There are times when we need to quietly listen to others and support what they do best. If we are sincere in this, others will support us when it is time to express our own strengths. Our strengths are then magnified because of the support we receive. We learn how and when to act without breaking harmony with others. Then, our actions no longer represent noise but contribute to beautiful, harmonious music.

Those who look for and support the strengths of others not only enhance their own lives but also help others to grow. We move toward living in a group or society filled with peace, love and respect, which further enhances everyone's strengths. Our happiness deepens, and life becomes a joy. Let's strive to consider the big picture to determine the right time, right place, right words and right actions so we can find harmony and balance within our own life's orchestra and make beautiful music every day.

peace breathing meditation

Peace Breathing Meditation is an easy-to-practice form of meditation suited to today's hectic lifestyles. It is based on scientific principles and is not associated with a religion. Peace Breathing combines the vital energy of breath with the powerful energy of thought to calm your mind, reduce your stress and open your heart to your true self. Peace Breathing can also be used as Moving Meditation, a wonderful way to defuse stressful situations as they occur in daily life.

The basic Peace Breathing method is
Inhale thinking "World," Exhale thinking "Peace"
While appearing to be quite simple, it took the Peace School's founder, Charles Kim's father, a lifetime of research into anatomy, brain functions, psychology and spirituality, and disciplined meditation for several hours every day, to create Peace Breathing. His goal was to develop a method that brought the same results as a strict meditation practice, yet was much more accessible to people in today's world. Peace Breathing takes the two most vital aspects

of human life—breath and thought—and binds them together to guide the mind to one's deeper self, the self that is connected to the vast, expansive harmony flowing throughout the universe.

Peace Breathing is so simple, yet so profound. Deep breathing is the first step. Breathing is our primary source of energy, yet most people have the habit of breathing shallowly. By slowing the breath down we provide a better oxygen supply to all the cells of the body. Most people have very busy and demanding lives, and over time the body has accepted tension and stress as being normal. Among other things, this means that the heart beats a little more quickly, blood vessels are more constricted, muscles are tense and the nervous system is in its fight-or-flight mode. Many of us have gotten used to having tension in our bodies so that the nervous system remains on alert even when we have down time. This is not healthy. Deep breathing itself is like a switch—a signal to the nervous system that it can relax. The body responds to this signal and relaxes, too. In times when we need to be on alert, deep breathing helps us to remain calm and think clearly so we can quickly take appropriate action. Of the many benefits of deep breathing, recent studies show that regular practice helps reduce stress, improve immune system functioning and enhance sleep. In particular, students experience reduced test anxiety and see improvements in academic performance.

So, deep breathing is the first step. The next step is peaceful thinking. This is based on the fact that all thoughts are recorded in the subconscious mind. Thoughts create energy (vibration or brain waves) and the type of thought we have creates that same type of energy (i.e., an angry thought creates angry energy; a compassionate thought creates compassionate energy, etc.). The more we repeat thoughts, the more they accumulate in our subconscious mind, and the more likely that type of energy will flow back to our conscious mind. So by repeating the thought of "World Peace," we build the energy of peace within our own mind, we set the stage for peace to come back to us in the future, and we emit the energy or vibration of peace to the world. This is fundamental to creating lasting and sustainable peace for ourselves and for our planet.

Peace Breathing connects us to our deeper self—free from limitations, judgments, boundaries or negative influences. With consistent practice our conscious mind remains in harmony with the energy of our true self. Then we become open to new possibilities, gain a wider perspective on issues, feel a connection to nature and to humanity, make decisions more easily and find that we naturally trust ourselves.

Peace Breathing Practice

When we breathe shallowly we are most likely breathing primarily from the chest. The breath becomes deeper when we make more use of the diaphragm by breathing from the stomach or abdomen. This means that when you inhale, the stomach/abdomen expands (gently pushes out) and when you exhale, the stomach/abdomen contracts (gently pushes in). If this movement is comfortable for you, try it with your Peace Breathing practice. If you are not accustomed to it, practice for several weeks by simply slowing down your normal breathing. Once this slower breathing pace becomes quite comfortable, begin slowly and gently pushing your stomach out as you inhale and gently moving it back in as you exhale. Later, when this begins to feel normal, you can practice the same movement from the abdomen.

When you practice Peace Breathing in a chair or other seated position, close your eyes and try to keep your back straight. You can also practice lying down for deep relaxation. This is especially helpful when you have trouble sleeping. When you are involved in your daily activities and feel tense, Peace Breathing is an excellent tool to use for Moving Meditation. Do moving Peace Breathing with your eyes open, at a comfortable pace according to whatever else you are doing, and continue to go about your day. In each case, breathe in and out through your nose. If this is not possible, breathe as quietly as possible through your mouth. Everyone can do Peace Breathing. Give it a try.

Peace Breathing
1 Rest your hands in your lap or in a comfortable position.
2 Close your eyes and begin to notice the inner movement of your breath.
3 Slow the pace down, but keep it comfortable.
4 Inhale slowly and quietly, thinking "World."
5 Pause for a moment.
6 Exhale slowing and quietly, thinking "Peace."
7 Repeat seven times or more.

Practice daily. When you are comfortable with seven breaths, increase the number of breaths gradually. It is more important to practice daily rather than to do Peace Breathing infrequently for long periods of time. Don't worry about how long you "should" practice or how slow your breath "should" be. The main point is to practice consistently, at your own pace. Remember to use Moving Meditation daily, too. Practice Peace Breathing as you walk, ride the bus, study, wait in line, cook, drive and especially during the "in between" times of your day. Breathe *World… Peace, World…Peace, World…Peace…*

Advanced Deep Breathing Technique
For people who wish to go further in their Peace Breathing practice or who have more experience in meditation, the following is a more advanced deep breathing method. As you become more comfortable with deep breathing, you no longer have to place your hand on your stomach or abdomen.

1 Place one hand on your stomach or abdomen. Close your eyes
2 As you inhale, thinking "World," let your stomach or abdomen move out. This is a gentle motion.
3 Pause for a moment.
4 As you exhale, thinking "Peace," let your stomach or abdomen gently move in.
5 Repeat seven times.
6 Rest your hands in your lap.
7 Continue breathing as above, seven times or more.

about the peace school

The Peace School is a non-profit, 501(c)(3) educational organization founded in Chicago in 1972 by MyungSu YuSung Kim, Charles Kim's father. The elder Kim felt that education for the 21st century must address the desperate need for peace on both an individual and global scale. He established his first educational organization in Korea in the 1950's and later brought his work to the United States. He founded The Peace School with the mission of helping people of all ages practice peace in everyday life. He firmly believed that by attaining peace in mind, body and spirit, an individual person creates strong, peaceful energy which forms the foundation for a broader peace in our families, schools, communities, nations and the world.

The Peace School teaches a unique blend of Peace Breathing Meditation, Peace Yoga, Traditional Tae Kwon Do and other practices for adults and children, with modified programs for seniors and nursing home residents. Within The Peace School, Charles Kim is referred to as Master Kim. His father, known as Grand Master Kim, is the founder of the Peace Breathing method.

The Peace School originated Peace Day in Chicago in 1978 and since then has organized annual public Peace Day celebrations, supported by each of the city's mayors since its inception. In 1987 the United Nations honored The Peace School as a *Peace Messenger* organization for its significant and concrete contributions to peace. The Peace School is home to the Chicago Build the Peace Committee which was formed in 2008 to commemorate Peace Day's 30th anniversary in Chicago and build upon this important work. The Committee partners with others, including Chicago Public Schools, City Colleges of Chicago, the Consular Corps of Chicago and cultural institutions across the city, to mainstream a Culture of Peace in Chicago.

charles h.c. kim

Hwi Chul Kim was born in Kwang Ju, South Korea in 1953 and lived in Seoul during much of his childhood. He took the name Charles when he became a naturalized U.S. citizen in 1980. Kim began sitting in on his parents' morning meditations when he was in elementary school and has continued daily meditation practice throughout his life. Weak and in poor health as a child, Kim joined yoga and martial art classes at his father's main *do jang* and within a year felt healthy enough to begin more intensive practice. Kim learned to reach beyond his physical power to persevere through the rigorous training with men twice his size. By the time he was in his early teens Kim became perhaps the youngest martial art instructor of his time.

In 1972 Kim and his parents, three sisters and brother moved to Chicago where he finished high school and helped his father set up and run The Peace School. He is a 9th degree black belt. Kim holds a Bachelors of Actuarial Mathematics from Northeastern Illinois University and a Masters of Computer Science from DePaul University. Since 1981 he has worked as an information technology professional for a large Chicago financial institution. He and his wife, Jennifer, live on Chicago's north side.

After his father's passing in 1999, Kim became President of The Peace School. He oversees the School's operations and teaches Peace Breathing Meditation, Peace Yoga and Traditional Tae Kwon Do. He also conducts Peace Breathing Meditation seminars. Kim is a firm believer in consistent practice and applying methods for creating peace in daily life, not just understanding theories or accumulating knowledge. He is an engaging and intuitive speaker using vivid stories, examples from nature, experiences in the workplace and other illustrations of how we can bring peace to ourselves and to the world.

For more information about The Peace School or Peace Breathing classes and seminars, visit the website or contact:

The Peace School
International Association for World Peace
3121 North Lincoln Avenue
Chicago, IL 60657-3111
Phone: 773.248.7959
www.peaceschool.org
info@peaceschool.org

To hear a Peace Breathing audio, click on *meditation* under the *classes* heading on the website.

Made in the USA
Lexington, KY
28 July 2019